BIBLE COPY WORK

BOOK 1

PROVERBS
CHAPTERS 1 - 3

COMPILED AND ILLUSTRATED BY EMILY A.

Bible Copy Work: Book One Proverbs Chapters One - Three

Copyright 2025 by Emily A. Pope

All rights reserved

No part of this work may be reproduced or transmitted in any form or by any means, electronic or mechanical, including photocopying and recording, or by any information storage or retrieval system, except as may be expressly permitted by the 1976 Copyright Act or in writing from the publisher. Requests for permission can be addressed to Inscript Books, a division of Dove Christian Publishers, P.O. Box 611, Bladensburg, MD 20710-0611, www.inscriptpublishing.com.

Paperback ISBN 978-1-957497-53-2

Inscript and the portrayal of a pen with script are trademarks of Dove Christian Publishers.

Published in the United States of America

Unless otherwise noted, all Scripture quotations are taken from the King James Version of the Bible. (Public Domain.)

TABLE OF LESSONS

Introduction v

Instructions vi

Lesson 1
Chapter 1 Verse 1 1

Lesson 2
Chapter 1 Verse 2 1

Lesson 3
Chapter 1 Verse 3 2

Lesson 4
Chapter 1 Verse 4 3

Lesson 5
Chapter 1 Verse 5 3

Lesson 6
Chapter 1 Verse 6 4

Lesson 7
Chapter 1 Verse 7 5

Lesson 8
Chapter 1 Verse 8 5

Lesson 9
Chapter 1 Verse 9 6

Lesson 10
Chapter 1 Verse 10 7

Lesson 11
Chapter 1 Verse 11 7

Lesson 12
Chapter 1 Verse 12 8

Lesson 13
Chapter 1 Verse 13 9

Lesson 14
Chapter 1 Verse 14 9

Lesson 15
Chapter 1 Verse 15 10

Lesson 16
Chapter 1 Verse 16 11

Lesson 17
Chapter 1 Verse 17 11

Lesson 18
Chapter 1 Verse 18 12

Lesson 19
Chapter 1 Verse 19 13

Lesson 20
Chapter 1 Verse 20 13

Lesson 21
Chapter 1 Verse 21 14

Lesson 22
Chapter 1 Verse 22 15

Lesson 23
Chapter 1 Verse 23 15

Lesson 24
Chapter 1 Verse 24 16

Lesson 25
Chapter 1 Verse 25 17

Lesson 26
Chapter 1 Verse 26 17

Lesson 27
Chapter 1 Verse 27 18

Lesson 28
Chapter 1 Verse 28 19

Lesson 29
Chapter 1 Verse 29 19

Lesson 30
Chapter 1 Verse 30 20

Lesson 31
Chapter 1 Verse 31 21

Lesson 32
Chapter 1 Verse 32 21
Lesson 33
Chapter 1 Verse 33 22
Lesson 34
Chapter 2 Verses 1 – 2 23
Lesson 35
Chapter 2 Verses 3 – 4 24
Lesson 36
Chapter 2 Verses 5 – 6 25
Lesson 37
Chapter 2 Verses 7 – 8 26
Lesson 38
Chapter 2 Verses 9 – 10 27
Lesson 39
Chapter 2 Verses 11 – 12 28
Lesson 40
Chapter 2 Verses 13 – 14 29
Lesson 41
Chapter 2 Verses 15 – 16 30
Lesson 42
Chapter 2 Verses 17 – 18 31
Lesson 43
Chapter 2 Verses 19 – 20 32
Lesson 44
Chapter 2 Verses 21 – 22 33
Lesson 45
Chapter 3 Verses 1 – 2 34
Lesson 46
Chapter 3 Verses 3 – 4 35
Lesson 47
Chapter 3 Verses 5 – 6 36
Lesson 48
Chapter 3 Verses 7 – 8 37
Lesson 49
Chapter 3 Verses 9 – 10 38
Lesson 50
Chapter 3 Verses 11 – 12 39
Lesson 51
Chapter 3 Verses 13 – 14 40
Lesson 52
Chapter 3 Verses 15 – 16 41
Lesson 53
Chapter 3 Verses 17 – 18 42
Lesson 54
Chapter 3 Verses 19 – 20 43
Lesson 55
Chapter 3 Verses 21 – 22 44
Lesson 56
Chapter 3 Verses 23 – 24 45
Lesson 57
Chapter 3 Verses 25 – 26 46
Lesson 58
Chapter 3 Verses 27 – 28 47
Lesson 59
Chapter 3 Verses 29 – 30 48
Lesson 60
Chapter 3 Verses 31 – 32 49
Lesson 61
Chapter 3 Verses 33 – 35 50

INTRODUCTION

I grew up in a home where the Lord and His word were first and foremost in all of our education, as they should be.

My mother had us copy out of the Bible; when we were young, we copied from the McGuffey's Readers. Once we were old enough to copy the small words in our Bibles, that is where we went for our daily copy work, specifically to Proverbs and Psalms, which I wore out in my own Bible through my copying of them!

I intend to continue this tradition with my own children someday, but I would like them to be able to copy from the Bible from the youngest age possible without having to use the McGuffey's Reader (which is still a wonderful source of reading).

To this end, I would like to introduce "Bible Copy Work: Book 1." It is simply a copy of the KJV Bible with the words slightly larger and pictures to go along with each verse. I intended to do this for my own children, but as a writer, I believe I am called to share all I can with others, even if it is in such a small way as a copy work book.

I pray that this will be a wonderful resource for parents who want their children to be covered in the word of God in every detail of their lives. For if they are going to become acquainted with the written word, why should they not do so through the greatest book ever written and the only one inspired by the One who made them.

Emily A.

INSTRUCTIONS

The use of this book is simple; the child should read the verse of the lesson they are on, or the parent should read it to them if they themselves cannot. The child should then be given a notebook and encouraged to write his or her name at the top of their notebook along with the date. They can write "Bible Copy Work" at the top as well, and under that, the chapter and verse they are copying in that lesson. Then they should copy the verse exactly as it is printed, with care given to good penmanship. The parent should then check for correct spelling and grammar. Copy work is simply an exercise to build a foundation of correct grammar and spelling, and I believe the Bible is the best place to learn this. Even if some of the words to copy seem a little old to us; perhaps we have lost too many of the old ways of speaking and it is time to bring them back.

This book is meant for ages 7 – 8.

Copy Work should be done every other day; this book should be done within 1 year.

Lesson 1

-

Chapter 1 Verse 1

The Proverbs of Solomon the son
of David, king of Israel;

Lesson 2

-

Chapter 1 Verse 2

To know wisdom and instruction; to perceive
The words of understanding;

Lesson 3

-

Chapter 1 Verse 3

To receive the instruction of wisdom, justice, and judgment, and equity;

Lesson 4

-

Chapter 1 Verse 4

To give subtilty to the simple, to the young man knowledge and discretion.

Lesson 5

-

Chapter 1 Verse 5

A wise man will hear, and will increase learning; and a man of understanding shall attain unto wise counsels:

Lesson 6

-

Chapter 1 Verse 6

To understand a proverb, and the interpretation; the words of the wise, and their dark sayings.

Lesson 7

Chapter 1 Verse 7

The fear of the Lord is the beginning of knowledge: but fools despise wisdom and instruction.

Lesson 8

Chapter 1 Verse 8

My son, hear the instruction of thy father, and forsake not the law of thy mother:

Lesson 9

-

Chapter 1 Verse 9

For they shall be an ornament of grace unto thy head, and chains about thy neck.

Lesson 10

-

Chapter 1 Verse 10

My son, if sinners entice thee,
consent thou not.

Lesson 11

-

Chapter 1 Verse 11

If they say, Come with us,
let us lay wait for blood, let us
lurk privily for the innocent without cause:

Lesson 12

-

Chapter 1 Verse 12

Let us swallow them up alive as the grave;

and whole, as those

that go down into the pit:

Lesson 13

-

Chapter 1 Verse 13

We shall find all precious substance,
we shall fill our houses with spoil:

Lesson 14

-

Chapter 1 Verse 14

Cast in thy lot among us;
let us all have one purse:

Lesson 15

-

Chapter 1 Verse 15

My son, walk not thou in
the way with them;
refrain thy foot from their path:

Lesson 16

-

Chapter 1 Verse 16

For their feet run to evil,
and make haste to
shed blood.

Lesson 17

-

Chapter 1 Verse 17

Surely in vain the net is
spread in the sight of any bird.

Lesson 18

-

Chapter 1 Verse 18

And they lay wait for their own blood;
they lurk privily for their own lives.

Lesson 19

-

Chapter 1 Verse 19

So are the ways of every one that is greedy
of gain; which taketh away the life
of the owners thereof.

Lesson 20

-

Chapter 1 Verse 20

Wisdom crieth without; she uttereth
her voice in the streets:

Lesson 21

-

Chapter 1 Verse 21

She crieth in the chief place of concourse, in the openings of the gates: in the city she uttereth her words, saying,

Lesson 22

-

Chapter 1 Verse 22

How long, ye simple ones, will ye love simplicity? and the scorners delight in their scorning, and fools hate knowledge?

Lesson 23

-

Chapter 1 Verse 23

Turn you at my reproof: behold,
I will pour out my spirit unto you,
I will make known my words unto you.

Lesson 24

-

Chapter 1 Verse 24

Because I have called, and ye refused;

I have stretched out my hand,

and no man regarded;

Lesson 25

-

Chapter 1 Verse 25

But ye have set at
nought all my counsel,
and would none of my reproof:

Lesson 26

-

Chapter 1 Verse 26

I also will laugh at your calamity;
I will mock when your fear cometh;

Lesson 27

-

Chapter 1 Verse 27

When your fear cometh as desolation, and your destruction cometh as a whirlwind; when distress and anguish cometh upon you.

Lesson 28

-

Chapter 1 Verse 28

Then shall they call upon me,
but I will not answer; they shall seek
me early, but they shall not find me:

Lesson 29

-

Chapter 1 Verse 29

For that they hated knowledge,
and did not choose the
fear of the LORD:

Lesson 30

-

Chapter 1 Verse 30

They would none of my counsel:
they despised all my reproof.

Lesson 31

-

Chapter 1 Verse 31

Therefore shall they eat of the fruit of their own way, and be filled with their own devices.

Lesson 32

-

Chapter 1 Verse 32

For the turning away of the simple shall slay them, and the prosperity of fools shall destroy them.

Lesson 33

-

Chapter 1 Verse 33

But whoso hearkeneth unto
me shall dwell
safely, and shall be quiet
from fear of evil.

Lesson 34

-

Chapter 2 Verses 1 – 2

My son, if thou wilt
receive my words, and hide
my commandments with thee;

So that thou incline thine ear
unto wisdom, and apply
thine heart to understanding;

Lesson 35

-

Chapter 2 Verses 3 – 4

Yea, if thou criest after knowledge,
and liftest up thy voice
for understanding;

If thou seekest her as
silver, and searchest for her as
for hid treasures;

Lesson 36

-

Chapter 2 Verses 5 – 6

Then shalt thou understand the fear of the LORD, and find the knowledge of God.

For the LORD giveth wisdom: out of his mouth cometh knowledge and understanding.

Lesson 37

-

Chapter 2 Verses 7 – 8

He layeth up sound wisdom
for the righteous: he is a
buckler to them that walk uprightly.

He keepeth the paths of judgment,
and preserveth the way
of his saints.

Lesson 38

Chapter 2 Verses 9 – 10

Then shalt thou understand
righteousness, and judgment, and equity;
yea, every good path.

When wisdom entereth into
thine heart, and knowledge
is pleasant unto thy soul;

Lesson 39

Chapter 2 Verses 11 – 12

Discretion shall preserve thee,
understanding shall
keep thee:

To deliver thee from the way of
the evil man, from the man
that speaketh forward things;

Lesson 40

Chapter 2 Verses 13 – 14

Who leave the paths of
uprightness, to walk
in the ways of darkness;

Who rejoice to do evil,
and delight in the frowardness
of the wicked;

Lesson 41

Chapter 2 Verses 15 – 16

Whose ways are crooked,
and they
froward in their paths:

To deliver thee from the
strange woman, even from the stranger
which flattereth with her words;

Lesson 42

Chapter 2 Verses 17 – 18

Which forsaketh the guide of her youth, and forgetteth the covenant of her God.

For her house inclineth unto death, and her paths unto the dead.

Lesson 43

-

Chapter 2 Verses 19 – 20

None that go unto her
return again,
neither take they hold of the paths
of life.

That thou mayest walk in
the way of good men, and
keep the paths of the righteous.

Lesson 44

Chapter 2 Verses 21 – 22

For the upright shall dwell in the land, and the perfect shall remain in it.

But the wicked shall be cut off from the earth, and the transgressors shall be rooted out of it.

Lesson 45

Chapter 3 Verses 1 – 2

My son, forget not my law;
but let thine heart
keep my commandments:

For length of days,
and long life, and peace,
shall they add to thee.

Lesson 46

Chapter 3 Verses 3 – 4

Let not mercy and truth
forsake thee:
bind them about thy neck;
write them upon the table of thine heart:

So shalt thou find favour
and good understanding in the
sight of
God and man.

Lesson 47

Chapter 3 Verses 5 – 6

Trust in the LORD with
all thine heart;
and lean not unto thine
own understanding.

In all thy ways acknowledge him,
and he shall direct thy paths.

Lesson 48

Chapter 3 Verses 7 – 8

Be not wise in thine
own eyes: fear the LORD,
and depart from evil.

It shall be health to thy
navel, and marrow to thy bones.

Lesson 49

Chapter 3 Verses 9 – 10

Honour the Lord with thy substance, and with the firstfruits of all thine increase:

So shall thy barns be filled with plenty, and thy presses shall burst out with new wine.

Lesson 50

Chapter 3 Verses 11 – 12

My son, despise not the
chastening of the LORD; neither
be weary of his correction:

For whom the LORD loveth
he correcteth; even as a father the son
in whom he delighteth.

Lesson 51

-

Chapter 3 Verses 13 – 14

Happy is the man that
findeth wisdom, and the man
that getteth understanding.

For the merchandise of it is
better than the merchandise of silver,
and the gain thereof than fine gold.

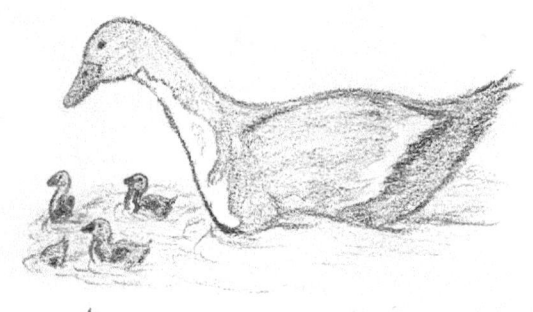

Lesson 52

Chapter 3 Verses 15 – 16

She is more precious than rubies:
and all the things thou canst
desire are not to be
compared unto her.

Length of days is in her
right hand; and in her left hand
riches and honour.

Lesson 53

-

Chapter 3 Verses 17 – 18

Her ways are ways of pleasantness,
and all her paths are peace.

She is a tree of life to them
that lay hold upon her: and
happy is every one that retaineth her.

Lesson 54

Chapter 3 Verses 19 – 20

The LORD by wisdom hath founded
the earth; by understanding hath
he established the heavens.

By his knowledge the depths
are broken up,
and the clouds drop down the dew.

Lesson 55

-

Chapter 3 Verses 21 – 22

My son, let not them depart
from thine eyes: keep
sound wisdom and discretion:

So shall they be life unto
thy soul, and grace to thy neck.

Lesson 56

Chapter 3 Verses 23 – 24

Then shalt thou walk in thy
way safely, and thy foot
shall not stumble.

When thou liest down, thou
shalt not be afraid: yea, thou shalt lie
down, and thy sleep shall be sweet.

Lesson 57

-

Chapter 3 Verses 25 – 26

Be not afraid of sudden fear, neither of the desolation of the wicked, when it cometh.

For the LORD shall be thy confidence, and shall keep thy foot from being taken.

Lesson 58

Chapter 3 Verses 27 – 28

Withhold not good from them to whom it is due, when it is in the power of thine hand to do it.

Say not unto thy neighbour, Go, and come again, and to morrow I will give; when thou hast it by thee.

Lesson 59

Chapter 3 Verses 29 – 30

Devise not evil against thy neighbour, seeing he dwelleth securely by thee.

Strive not with a man without cause, if he have done thee no harm.

Lesson 60

-

Chapter 3 Verses 31 – 32

Envy thou not the oppressor,
and choose none of
his ways.

For the froward is abomination
to the LORD: but his secret is with
the righteous.

Lesson 61

-

Chapter 3 Verses 33 – 35

The curse of the LORD is in

the house of the wicked: but

he blesseth the habitation of the just.

Surely he scorneth the scorners:

but he giveth grace unto the lowly.

The wise shall inherit glory:

but shame shall be

the promotion of fools.

www.ingramcontent.com/pod-product-compliance
Lightning Source LLC
Chambersburg PA
CBHW060407010526
44107CB00005B/608